GW01090276

LIVING AMAZED

Harnessing the Power of Journaling

Copyright

Endorsements

The best part of reading this book, Living Amazed- Harnessing the Power of journaling, is the fact that it is concise, easy to read and straight to the point. It is detailed enough for anyone who wants to start journaling and gives even more motivation for journaling veterans to keep going.

I will recommend this book to everyone, most especially women because sometimes, we need that space to sort through the many things going on in our minds from time to time. Well done for putting this great resource together, Detola.

Oluseye Ashiru,
CEO, Mom Youniversity
momyouniversity.com

Living Amazed- Harnessing the Power of journaling is an amazing guide for any woman looking to start or re-start their journaling journey. It offers practical tips, digestible guidelines, and inspirational examples that will ignite the fire within you.

Once again Detola has hit the nail on the head with this must read tool for Super Working Mums!

Mosope Idowu,
Founder, Bethel Fit Mum Inc.
www.bethelfitmum.com

Living Amazed- Harnessing the Power of journaling: wow! This book has rekindled my love for journaling. I have so many notebooks and journals waiting to be used, I even have an app that I used religiously for one year but I abandoned it. However, reading Detola's and the other ladies' experiences of journaling has encouraged me to go back and start small.

I love the simplicity Detola has used to share the core message behind journaling. I know this book will help a lot of women start journaling or rekindle the fire like it has for me. Thank you Detola and everyone who contributed.

Eloho Efemuai,
Broadcaster/Founder
Heartsong Live Radio
www.heartsonglive.co.uk/

Dedication

This book is dedicated to the women in the Super Working Mum Academy.

Thank you for allowing me to be a "midwife" to you, in birthing your God-given dreams.

Acknowledgements

My sincere thanks go to the following:

Abba Father for loving me and giving me the gift of writing, Jesus for redeeming my soul and Holy Spirit for breathing life into my writing.

Funmi Onamusi, Emilola Shyllon, Leigh Ann Napier, Jacqueline Ani, Toks Aruoture and Marion Palmer for agreeing to share your journaling experiences in this book. I enjoyed reading your stories and I know my readers would too!

Leigh Ann Napier, for adding your creativity to this book from the very get go.

Moyo, my super firstborn daughter, who graciously agreed to read over the book and do some final editing at short notice despite a very busy school schedule. I love you!

Tj, my darling husband, for being so supportive in allowing me to pursue my dreams.

Ola Thomas, my amazing Online Business Manager & friend, because you came into my life, I am able to operate more in my brilliant zone. You rock!

Olumide Saka, you creatively and patiently brought this book to life. Thank you.

The Super Working Mum Academy, every single one of you are talented and you make me proud. Thank you for your commitment to manifesting your God-given dreams. My "no drama" crew, I salute you.

The Super Working Mum community, all over the world. Because of you, the vision God gave me found expression. A big shout out to the one hundred and forty women who completed my journaling survey way back in 2015, which partly inspired the writing of this book.

Everyone who has prayed for me, believed in me and stood by me, I am grateful. If I begin to mention names I might go on and on forever but I am truly blessed to have you in my corner. May Abba reward you.

Table of Contents

Introduction 1

What is Journaling? 4

My Journaling Story 8

Benefits of Journaling 12

What time of day should I journal? 16

Must I journal every day? 18

What should I write in my journal? 20

Two Way Journaling With God 24

Six Journaling Experiences 28

Conclusion 52

Recommended Journals 56

Note from the Author 74

Foreword

"Let this be written for a future generation, that a people not yet created may praise the LORD" – Ps. 102:18 NIV

My husband and I had been married for four years and had been trying unsuccessfully to get pregnant for months. In between prayers and medical tests, we realised more and more that it would take a supernatural intervention. There were days I felt encouraged. Some days, I remember feeling so frustrated and helpless. Every month when my period came, I would feel like a failure. But we refused to give up.

One morning, while cleaning the house, I came across an old, green notebook stuck in between two larger books in a corner of the bedroom. I paused to pick it up and flipped through the pages. The topic "Strength to Conceive." caught my attention and I found myself being taken back to a time in my life. From the entry date, I was probably in my third or fourth year at the university. I had written this poem at 4 a.m. that day, probably one of those restless nights when I couldn't sleep and journaled instead. My notes focused on Sarah (Abraham's wife) and how despite all odds including her own unbelief, she received the strength to conceive. I ended the note that day with an impromptu 3-paragraph poem on how strength comes in the place of waiting.

Whaaaaat!!

I wrote those words a little over 10 years ago. Did God know we would have a delay in having kids in the future? Did He stir me up to pray into the future? Or was it to stir up my faith for such a time as this?

In that moment, when I needed encouragement, it was right there in my room. That's the power of journaling! I shifted from a place of stress and feeling overwhelmed to a place of harmony, calm, peace and joy. It allowed me to see my life with new eyes and to experience clarity of purpose through the waiting season of my life.

One of the life-changing tools Detola recommends for her clients and community is journaling. Journaling is a powerful tool that can help you to process your thoughts and feelings, set goals and intentions, and create positive change in your life. If you need a fresh start, a jumpstart, or you're looking for a proven way to transform your life, Detola's book and journals can help you to harness the power of journaling to make positive changes in your life.

There's a path that shines brighter every day
There's a resting place for the weary soul;
For his thoughts towards you are good continually
His plans, a cut-out strategy, unique to its purpose
What has he spoken about you, your future, and your impact?
Write.........

Mofoluwaso Ilevbare
Executive Leadership & Confidence Coach
www.mofoluwaso.com

Introduction

You are probably reading this book because you are new to journaling, you have heard about journaling but not experienced it, you have journaled in the past, or you are a veteran journal writer and want to learn more.

Whatever the case, I am sure by the time you are done reading you will be motivated to pick up the habit of journaling which has the potential to transform your life.

Many women I know complain about their feelings of overwhelm, stress, being stagnant, lack of clarity and direction. They sometimes lack purpose and motivation in life to manifest their big dreams. There are so many strategies and tools you can use to address these issues but one simple and free tool that can make a huge impact is journaling.

Journaling has helped me address these issues for many years now and in this book, I want to share with you why you should consider journaling. My story is proof that journaling can move you from a state of stress and overwhelm to a place of harmony, calm, peace and joy where you can experience clarity of purpose.

God has so much he wants to do through you! He has big dreams for you to manifest on earth. But when stress, overwhelm and confusion get in the way, you get distracted from your purpose. Journaling helps you stay on track and in tune with what God is saying.

The first time I heard the phrase Living Amazed was from Joyce Meyer, a woman of faith whom I deeply admire. She encourages believers to always remain amazed by what God is doing in their lives no matter how small it seems. This will help us live in the moment, enjoy life, and be more mindful.

I want to share with you how you can always live amazed, grow as a Kingdom woman and be a Super Working Mum simply by journaling.

I have invited six amazing women to share their journaling experiences with you, so you can see when they started journaling, what they journal about, and how it has helped them.

But before we go into all that, let's take a step back and discuss what journaling is, some of the benefits of journaling, and answer some questions I get asked often about journaling.

Later on, I will also share some obstacles in journaling and how to tackle them.

My hope and prayer is that after reading this book and the stories shared, you will be spurred on to start journaling yourself.

Enjoy!

'Detola Amure

What is Journaling?

Journaling is the act of writing your thoughts, experiences, and observations. It is a private space reserved just for you. It could be an account of your day like a diary.

From a spiritual point of view, it would involve writing what God is teaching you, your prayer requests, your gratitude and answers to prayers. It could include your hopes for the future, your dreams, or thoughts on a book you have read.

Writing in a journal is more than just writing facts or recounting events, it is an opportunity to write from your heart as you reflect on what God is saying, events, occurrences, and daily miracles in your life. It is a chance to get in touch with your inner self.

The word "journal" comes from the Latin word called diurnus meaning "of the day". People have kept journals since humans learnt to write. Famous people have enjoyed journaling including Leonardo da Vinci and Anne Frank. The Psalms in the Bible are accepted by many as David's prayer journal.

In today's world, there are various kinds of journals:
- **Prayer journals,** where you document your prayers and answer to prayers;
- **Prophecy journals,** where you document promises from God and/or prophetic words from others;
- **Gratitude journals,** where you list what you are grateful for;
- **Dream journals,** where you capture the dreams you have when you sleep;
- **Travel journals,** where you document your adventures;
- **Health and Fitness journals,** where you track your food, weight, energy etc.;
- **Goal journals,** where you track your goals to completions;

Or you could have a combination of any of the above or anything else for that matter. There are no hard and fast rules about what to write in your journal.

For the purposes of this book, we will focus on journaling for personal growth, including spiritual, emotional, and mental growth.

As wives and mothers, we deal with a lot on a daily basis. Sometimes our mind seems to want to explode!

Our husbands don't meet our expectations
Our children frustrate us
Our work is challenging
We can get a bit lost and wonder what our purpose is

We need an outlet where we can "dump" these multiple thoughts going through our heads.

Journaling is one way to:
- *Process and articulate your thoughts*
- *Talk to God and tell him how you feel*
- *Listen to God's thoughts and instructions*
- *Grow in your faith and document your journey.*

Sometimes your heart is heavy with all kinds of worry, but you are not sure how to pray. When that happens, you can write out your prayers instead. Your journal is a safe outlet where you can be real, with no fear of judgment or concern for what anyone else thinks.

Some people use their blogs or social media as a form of journaling. I kept a personal blog for about 6 years but I still find traditional journaling with pen and paper more therapeutic. Find what works for you. You don't have to be a talented writer to keep a journal: all you need is an open mind to let those words flow as you write.

My Journaling Story

Growing up as a teenager, I kept a diary (a form of a journal) in which I wrote almost every night about my day and my feelings. It was partially focused on me and partly focused on God. To be honest, it was probably more focused on me than God. It was about my thoughts, my feelings, my crushes, what someone said to me that upset me, etc.

When I was 14, I went to boarding school and stopped journaling for a number of years. A few years later, I picked up journaling occasionally when I needed an outlet to pour out what was on my mind. It wasn't until early 2014 that journaling became a big part of my life after I discovered the huge benefits I had been getting from my occasional journaling.

If journaling made me feel better, more peaceful, and calmer, why not make it an everyday thing? This time my journal was more focused on what God was saying to me, my prayer requests, answered prayers, my confessions/declarations and intention for the day and what God was doing in my life.

The middle of 2014 was a tough time for my family and me financially. I was also waiting on God for some direction on the next step to take in my life. It was a dark, confusing, and stressful time. I wrote furiously in my journal, willing God to take control. It was a year of trusting and holding on to God.

I remembered when we'd had a similar challenge two years earlier. I wrote about that experience in my journal and documented how God came through and the lessons I learned. It ended up being one phone call that changed our precarious situation. God reminded me of that challenging time and I heard Him clearly say to me He was going to change our circumstances again with just one simple action. I stood on that word and that kept my faith going. Even when things didn't seem to be physically changing, I knew God was working behind the scenes. This time it was one email that changed things around for my family.

This is just one of many examples of why I journal and why it has such an impact on my life. When I see God's hand in my life and in the life of my family especially during trying times, I write it all down. I write the lessons, I write about the experience, and I write about how God came through. It has become a case of living amazed by what God does on a daily basis. Knowing that HE cared for even the tiniest detail of my life and that He is my ever-present help in times of trouble is a great source of joy to me.

Writing about my experiences is a reminder never to take God for granted or forget what He has done for me. It is also an opportunity to remember what He has done in the past when challenging times come. He is the same yesterday, today, and forever and journaling gives me a powerful reminder that He will continue to come through for me. Journaling on a daily basis has helped me grow in my faith and mature emotionally and mentally as well.

Benefits of Journaling

I carried out a survey in the Super Working Mum community to understand women's experience with journaling and to have a feel for those who journal and those who don't. Over 140 women responded to the survey. It was interesting to find out that

- 52% of those who responded keep a journal while 48% don't journal due to one reason or the other.
- Of the 48% who don't journal, 32% said it was because they didn't see the benefit or importance while 30% said they didn't have the time to journal.
- 49% of responders said they would definitely give journaling a chance if they knew the importance or benefit and 46% would consider journaling.

I want women all over the world to experience the stress relief, clarity, and self-awareness that the practice of journaling provides. It also leaves you with the gift of having a record of building faith, strength and personal miracles in your life.

My heart-felt desire is that women feel the same impact that journaling has had in my life which is to Live Amazed every day.

Some benefits of journaling that I have experienced personally are:

- **Journaling has helped me to develop an attitude of thankfulness.** The first thing I write in my journal every morning is three things I am grateful for. Even when I am having a tough time, this helps me look beyond my issues to what God is doing in my life and in the life of my family. Writing out my gratitude list has helped me to live amazed every day.

- **Journaling has helped me articulate my thoughts and change my perspective.** It brings clarity. Sometimes, when my mind is bogged down with all kinds of things, there is a release I experience when I write it down and read it back to myself. I am able to view my thoughts more objectively and give meaning to what has been on my mind. Sometimes I am able to completely eradicate what I thought was a big issue just by writing it down.
- **Journaling helps me document my prayer requests and more importantly, keep a record of my praise report of answered prayers.** I mentioned earlier some of the answers to prayer God gave me & my family and how I was reassured when a new challenge came my way. I take comfort in what God has already done for me and believe Him for future concerns by building on my faith from the past.
- **Journaling helps me worry less.** I am always eager to write in my journal especially when I have a new challenge or issue because I believe God reads my journal and is waiting to surprise me with what He can do. I am expectant instead of worrying.
- **Journaling helps me desire to hear more from God and be closer to Him.** Because I am eager to write what God is sharing with me, I write expecting to hear from Him as I read His Word to get a personal word for the day.
- **My journal is a safe place, to be honest with myself and with God.** I can tell Him when I have messed up or what I am struggling with and I hear Him teach me how I can do better next time. This helps me know myself better and become a better version of myself. It deepens my relationship with God and with myself.

- **Journaling helps me slow down and live each day intentionally, full of hope and a good attitude.** At the start of each day, I write out a declaration in my journal to help set the tone of the day. Two of the declarations I like to write are: "This is the day that the Lord has made, I will rejoice and be glad in it," or "The Lord is my shepherd I lack nothing,". By writing out declarations and meditating on them, I am able to face each day with God's strength and not only rely on my abilities.

You can experience these benefits too if you give journaling a try.

What time of day should I journal?

Journaling is a personal experience, so make it your own! Whenever you can journal is the right time for you to journal! Many Christian women I know journal as part of their quiet time with God either early in the morning or in the evening before they go to bed. Some carry their journals around everywhere they go and will journal as they get a break throughout the day.

Early mornings are great because your mind is fresh. You can almost hear yourself thinking in the quiet and the words may flow more easily. Evenings are equally great because the events of the day are still fresh in your mind.

You can write down your experiences and what God revealed to you during the day. On-the-go journaling is a great way to capture experiences and feelings as they happen.

I tend to journal in the morning during my time with God. I also jot down words or inspirations that come to me during the day on my smartphone so I won't forget to record them later. The bottom line is, to find what works for you. If you are a morning person like me, journal in the morning. If you like to write to unwind just before going to bed, evenings might be the time for you. Or you could do both.

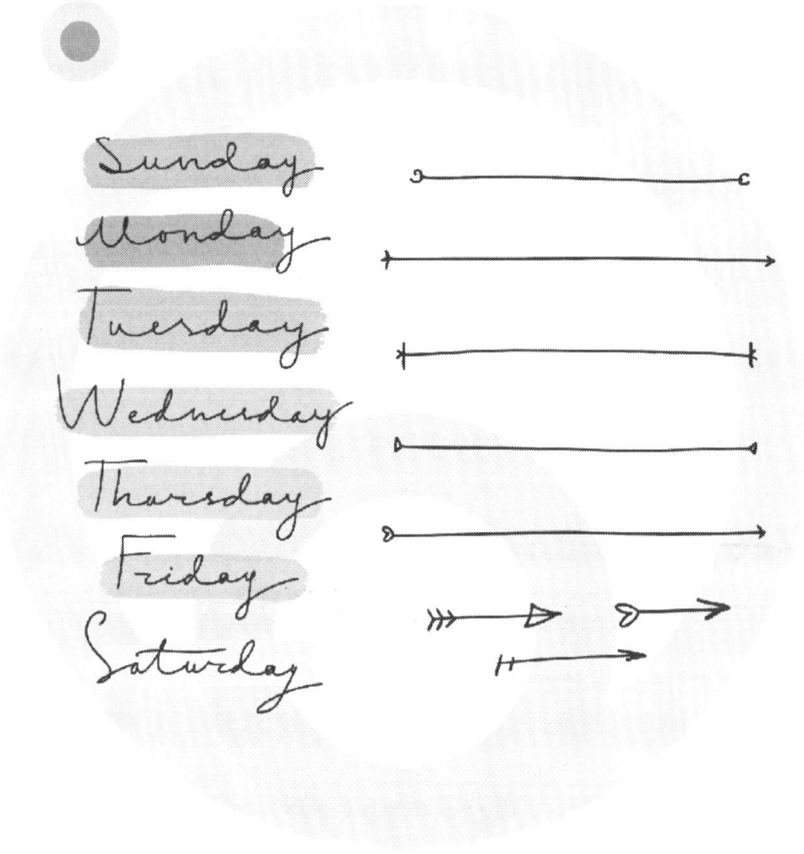

Sunday

Monday

Tuesday

Wednesday

Thursday

Friday

Saturday

Must I Journal Every day?

There are no rules for how often you should journal. If you are just starting out, then I suggest taking it one day at a time. Starting is the most important thing. With time you will get a feel of how often you should journal. It is what you make out of the experience, so don't feel under pressure to journal every day just because someone else does.

As I mentioned before, I have journaled on and off over the years. For some years I didn't journal at all. Then I picked it back up again and journaled when I felt like it, especially when my heart or mind was burdened and I needed to get things off my chest. However, with time, journaling has become part of my lifestyle just like the other Kingdom women you will read about later on in this book. The benefits I have experienced in my own life are too great for me not to journal every day.

What Should I Write in My Journal?

Now that we have looked at the benefits of journaling, you may still be wondering what to write inside your journal. I know people who have tons of beautiful journals on their bookshelves but they are yet to use any. Most times it is because they are not sure what to write.

First, get clear on your why. For most people, it is for their personal growth.

This can involve spiritual, emotional, mental and physical growth. To grow you need to know yourself and to know yourself, you need to know your thoughts. To know the quality of your thoughts, you need to write them down and read what you have written.

What you write in your journal is totally up to you with your "why" in mind. No one else will see it so it doesn't have to be fancy or neat, however, make sure you can read what you have written.

You can decide to journal:
- What God is saying to you;
- Prayers and answers;
- Questions and things you need clarity on;
- Your gratitude;
- Prophetic words from others;
- Dreams;
- Your diet and fitness journey;
- Goals and desires;
- Your daily activities;
- Travel adventures
- And more

It is not compulsory to have multiple journals, especially if you are just starting out. You can use one journal for everything.

I personally have different journals for different things as I find it easier to know where what is recorded. I don't make use of all of them every day, only as appropriate.

I have a journal to record my dreams, another to track my goals, another to record my prayers and answers, another for promises and prophetic words and another for two way journaling with God.

Two Way Journaling With God

One of my favourite ways of communicating with God is through what is known as two-way journaling. Two-way journaling is the practice of talking to God through writing and then recording what He says back to you.

In the past, I was used to writing out my prayers in my journal but that was a one-way communication which I found frustrating because I never waited to hear what God had to say to me. However, since I discovered two-way journaling, I now have a proper dialogue with God.

Two-way journaling involves writing down your prayers, thanksgiving, praise report, anxious thoughts, fears, confusing situations, questions etc. Then, you take the time to listen and write down whatever the Holy Spirit is saying to you concerning what you have written down.

Two-way journaling is a dynamic, powerful and supernatural interactive process that allows you to enjoy intimacy and friendship with God and encounter Him on a deeper level.

One easy way to start two-way journaling is to incorporate scripture. Read a portion of scripture, maybe a Psalm, personalise the scripture and then expand from there as Holy Spirit leads you.

For example, Psalm 23:1: The Lord is my shepherd, I shall not want.

Personalisation: *Because the Lord is my shepherd, I lack nothing. I have everything I need at all times. All my needs are always met, this is Abba's promise to me. The wisdom I need to parent my children is available to me. I know how to sort out that work situation. That pending bill is paid off. I have everything I need. The resources I need always show up at the right time.   Thank you, Father, because you never leave me stranded. I am so grateful and expectant!*

Two-way journaling with God has the potential to boost your confidence, and help you get your eyes off situations that seem bleak because you are focusing on God's thoughts concerning that challenge.

As you begin to make it a practice to involve God in your journaling, as you ask Him intentional questions, the words will begin to flow. Don't overthink it, just write and then once you are done, go over the words you have written to see what resonates with you.

Six Journaling Experiences

Now we will move on to the second part of this book, where I introduce to you six women, who have incorporated journaling into their lifestyle.

These are amazing Kingdom Women from different backgrounds, cultures, experiences, stories, and trials that are Living Amazed and harnessing the power of journaling to enhance their personal growth.

These women share their experiences with journaling and the impact it has had on their lives. They also share some tips for the busy woman on how to start journaling consistently.

Their answers are quite revealing and I hope you enjoy reading their stories like I did. Mostly, I hope their stories will inspire you to start journaling too!

"Journaling saved me from a depressive slump."

I originally started journaling in my first year in university. I belonged to a Christian Union fellowship and was inspired by the believers around me. I was hungry to hear from God too so I would wake up every morning, read my Bible and then document my thoughts, plans and ideas for the day. It was like a conversation journal and I used it to talk to God about anything and everything.

Back in my university days, I used to journal every day, but about five years later I stopped completely. I tried several times to restart journaling but never got beyond a few months at a time. In 2013, I lost my Dad and the sorrow sent me into a rather bad place emotionally and spiritually. I could not pray on my own anymore: I kept up appearances but was hollow inside.

I was reading a book by Courtney Joseph titled Women Living Well, and she recommended keeping a prayer journal and writing out your prayers. So I started journaling again but it was different this time - I needed to reconnect with God and doing so this way helped me. It was a very slow process but I am thankful today as that saved me from a depressive slump.

I can honestly say journaling (with the help of the Holy Spirit) helped me come back from a very terrible place and find my way back to a communion fellowship with God after the painful loss of my father.

When I journaled as a younger Christian, it taught me discipline and consistency. The process really helped me to keep aware of growing spiritually versus just keeping busy with church activities. Not the same thing!

In my journal now, I write my Bible reading for the day and my thoughts on that passage. I include prayer points - I have a prayer list organised by the day of the week, to help me remember to pray for everyone and not just my immediate family. I also try to write testimonies or things to be thankful for (I have to admit, I do not do this part on a regular basis).

My advice to anyone who wants to start journaling is simple: Do it! Start small - don't box yourself into a corner by trying to keep one 'type' of journal. When you start, do so with whatever you feel able to (thoughts, thanksgiving, prayers, devotional ...don't limit yourself). Also, be consistent. The more you journal, the more you will want to journal.

Journaling can help you in becoming more expressive and you will have a historical record of that process.

I know a lot of women say they do their devotional on the go or during lunchtime or at some point during the day. I am a strong believer in starting my day with the Lord and I find that if I don't journal in the morning, I can't do it for that day. So if you are a busy mum, I would say map out your day and analyse the hours you are asleep: Is there half an hour you could utilise better? Could you wake up earlier? Send the children to bed earlier so you can do it then? Could you find a quiet room for 30 minutes during lunch?

The possibilities are limitless...Find what works for you. If you set your mind to it you can find the time :-) Give it a try.

Funmi Onamusi is a wife and mother of 2 boys. She currently works as a Director in the National Health Service UK. Funmi is a working mum who is passionate about women retaining their God-given identity in a chaotic world of all pressures without giving up on the goal to be a Proverbs 31 woman as they continue their walk with God. Funmi is a published author and has written four books.

"Journaling has been a great source of healing."

I started journaling when I was diagnosed with depression in 2000. Journaling helped me write down my thoughts, but also write down the true thoughts that God has towards me - His thoughts towards me are thoughts of good and not evil. I would meditate on these thoughts to set me free from the thoughts of depression that would flood my mind.

Over the years, journaling has been a great source of healing for me and it has also helped me teach others how to heal as they journal.

*I had a dream where I was given a beautifully wrapped gift, and when I opened it, I saw a pair of beautiful 'His and Hers' burgundy ball pens, and I knew it was God showing me that I was called to write. During the same period, I was also given a verse: **Jeremiah 30:2-3**.*

The word that came to Jeremiah from the Lord: "Thus says the Lord, the God of Israel: Write in a book all the words that I have spoken to you. For behold, days are coming, declares the Lord, when I will restore the fortunes of my people, Israel and Judah, says the Lord, and I will bring them back to the land that I gave to their fathers, and they shall take possession of it."

Over the years this scripture has become a reality in my life where journaling is concerned. Every process and circumstance that God has taken me through has become a reason for me to journal so that I can use my learning in the process to set others free. As a result, the majority of my journals have now become chapters of books to empower, develop and provide nuggets for transformation and living life abundantly.

Journaling is a part of reflection. Reflection helps to identify areas where we have developed, it opens our minds to the aspect of transformation which is a huge area of positive change. As a university lecturer, I teach my students the importance of reflecting and journaling their learning.

When you journal what you're learning, it helps you understand the steps to heal in every area of your life. It opens your mind to think outside of the confinements of your own understanding and creates opportunities to reach a bigger community and finally, it enables you to bless others with wisdom and nuggets to life.

I journal almost every day, mostly early in the morning or before bedtime. In my journal, I write the revelations (light bulb moments) God gives me through some of the processes I am going through. When I go back to read my journals from previous years, especially the ones with light bulb moments, it makes more sense because I have matured over the years and the life experiences I've undergone confirm what was initially journaled.

Journaling has enabled me to publish 3 books, with another two still in the process of being written. I have also developed my own signature programs through journaling.

Journaling encourages me to release the thoughts and plans in my heart and that makes me walk in wholeness, hence the need to continue.

My advice to anyone who wants to start journaling is to start light. Nowadays, there are many ways to record your reflection, and that is by audio or video recording and of course writing.

My final nugget is, if you dream, make sure you have a journal by your bedside because those ideas have the potential to become great in the world.

Jacqueline Ani is a Transformational Leadership Consultant, Career Coach, Adult Literacy Lecturer, Inspirational Speaker and Author of three books. Her mission is to empower women to be successful in every area of their lives.

Jacqueline is the founder of Jacqueline Ani International and The Mentoring Group for International Women. She is also the Managing Director of Ani Recruitment, Training Consultancy, the Chief Editor of Women Empowering Women Magazine and Radio Presenter of Women Empowering Women Lifestyle Talk Show. She is also a fellow member of the School of Social Entrepreneurs.

Jacqueline has overcome many obstacles in life and uses these as strategies to help and build other women to fulfil their life's purpose. She operates as a midwife and prophet. You can connect with Jacqueline at https://www.jacquelineaniinternational.org/

"When I go a day or two without journaling, I feel 'off'."

I've been journaling since I was little. I think my first try at journaling was to record the adventures on a family vacation. I've journaled regularly since graduating from college. Now, I mainly journal prayers to record my neediness and His faithfulness. It also helps me stay focused and not fall asleep while I pray which serves that practical purpose. Ha! I love having a record of answered prayers.

I journal daily, first thing in the morning. My journal entries include gratitude, needs, praises, and things I hope to accomplish that day. Journaling has impacted my life greatly. It is a record of my conversation with God. It helps me focus on what is most important and I can get clarity on my thoughts as I write them down.

I know when I go a day or two without journaling, I feel "off". It really helps me have clarity and focus. Also, I don't have the best memory in the world so I love having a record to refer back to later.

Journaling doesn't have to be complicated if you are thinking of starting. You could just pick three bullet points to record each day to get started such as:

1) What are you grateful for?

2) What are you dreaming about?

3) What are you going to do today to move you closer to those dreams and goals?

As a busy mum who is not sure she can find the time to journal, I suggest you keep your journal with you to make any waiting time productive. You can use that "dead time" to write and reflect as well as prepare for what is ahead.

You matter. When you don't take time to think about and write about what matters to you, you can start to "disappear" as your own person. Being someone's wife and someone's mother is a high calling but knowing who you are and what you are about is critical in becoming the best you possible. No one else is responsible for your happiness. You have to recognise what makes you feel joyful, energised, & fulfilled. Journaling helps you discover all of these and so much more.

Leigh Ann Napier is a hand lettering artist/ modern calligrapher. She began her love of hand lettering as a way to memorise scripture in her journaling Bible. Before she knew it, her friends & family were asking her to do her "pretty words" on cards, canvas, wood, and walls! She calls herself an accidental entrepreneur but strives to be intentional in living a life she loves serving & encouraging as many people as possible along the way.

Leigh Ann is a published author, and has a life/ business coaching background but is happiest when she is creating art, singing, and hanging out with her family.

Leigh Ann lives in Lexington, KY with her husband, three amazing daughters, and her two rescue dogs, Macy & Westin. You can find her on Facebook at "Leigh Ann Napier Hand Lettering."

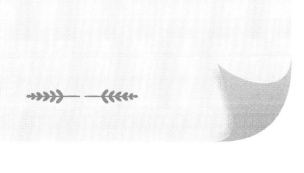

"Books and devotionals have sprung out of my journaling."

I started journaling aged 12 and it was a tool to manage my emotions. I journal every couple of days. That regularity is sometimes affected by extremely busy periods but before long, I start to feel overwhelmed and I know I need to pick up my pen. I tend to journal in the morning and late at night as part of my devotions.

In my journal, I include my prayers in bullet points and in full written expressions. I write down my desires for the future. I also include insights from Bible Reading & study times. I record significant dreams, prophetic words that I give to others and those I receive. I also note down my testimonies.

I have found journaling to be a very effective tool in managing and dealing with the daily stress of juggling home, work, ministry/business and life in general. It is sometimes the first thing that gets pushed aside when pressures build but rarely am I able to deal with those pressures without returning to journaling.

Journaling has been a tangible way of measuring and seeing spiritual growth in my life. Books and devotionals have sprung out of my journaling.

Journaling reminds me of the ways God has helped me and my loved ones, far and near.

When I struggle to pray or write or when I lack joy, re-reading previous journal entries helps me to refocus on God's love and goodness. Journaling is definitely a part of my lifestyle and I don't see myself ever not journaling.

For anyone reading this new to journaling, I want to let you know that you won't go wrong by journaling. Start now and don't get distracted by what it ought to look like. Just write down sincerely from where you are.

One of the best things to do is to journal as part of your devotions (Bible reading, praying, meditating) for often the Holy Spirit drops insights into your mind and your spirit in that space.

Elevate journaling to soul care and you'll find that you will make time for it. Even if it means letting go of other things which do not serve you well. The potential for journals to impact the lives of those who keep them and future generations cannot be overemphasised!

Emilola is a lover of life-giving words. She is first, a woman evolving in the truth of God's words. At her core, she believes in leaving people refreshed, whether that expresses itself through her writings or her many creative interests.

Emilola is a writer, poet, interior stylist & speaker among many other things. She has authored 31-day devotionals, journals and a deck of encouragement cards, the latter two being part of the Desired- Not -Abandoned (DNA) brand.

She is married, blessed with two children and creates an oasis for the soul at her blog site: www.thewellspringplace.com.

"To not journal is to not live"

I started journaling as early as age 6. My mum always kept a diary so I was pretty much born into it :). I journal now about 4 to 6 times a week, mostly early in the morning. Occasionally I get inspired or gifted with a lesson I have to write down immediately so I grab my journal, or phone depending on my proximity to either.

I include prayers, lessons, fears, plans and goals in my journal. I also self-coach myself out of challenging situations by writing, and of course, I vent.

Sometimes when I feel overwhelmed with an excessive amount of thoughts, I empty my mind on paper to get them out and rearrange them. I then pick up what's needed and toss out the junk.

Journaling helps me to get things done when I'm in a bind. It helps me to see things clearly when I'm confused or uncertain. Journaling has also helped to instil good habits in me - I adopt a new habit and when I come back to write, my journal pretty much asks if I've stayed true to it.

Journaling is intrinsically woven into the fabric of my being. To not journal is to not live. In order to grow, to thine own self be true. Your journal is one place no one else will visit but you, so you have an opportunity to be completely honest with yourself on paper. This helps to identify strengths and weaknesses which will propel or hinder you to great heights.

My advice for the busy mum who wants to start journaling is to make a weekly appointment with yourself to do some journaling. Make it a special time, with candles, peace and quiet, etc. if you wish. That way, you look forward to it. There is no pressure to fill the page, even if all you put down are the wins you had that week. You can also write one thing you're thankful for every few days. It is therapy!

Our minds carry and process millions of thoughts daily. As a man thinks, so he is - journaling exposes your own thoughts to you, this will help you to rediscover and fall in love with yourself.

Toks Aruoture is a mindset strategist, nursery interior designer and founder of The Baby Cot Shop in Chelsea, London. Toks believes that the most valuable tools for exponential growth are the gifts each person carries, but limiting beliefs often envelop them, which makes accessing their exceptional abilities difficult. Through her podcast, Living Inside Out, she helps women unwrap their gifts so they can play bigger. She is a prolific writer and sought-after speaker, and she is married with four sons. You can connect with Toks on her website: https://toksaruoture.com/

"Journaling- an encouragement for the future"

I've been journaling now for 40 years, so from that statement alone, you will gather that I regard it as an important part of a Christian's life! When I first started in January 1982, I had been married for nearly five years and was looking after two little ones aged two & a half and 16 months. A third child would be added to our family in 1983. It was a blessing that I did not have to work outside the home, although caring for little ones is full-time in itself!

My first entry said this: "After nearly seven years as a Christian I have at last begun something that should have started when I gave my heart to the Lord in 1975 – a diary of events, inspiration, prayers, indeed all that encompasses the development and growth of a Christian's life – not as a hankering for the past, but encouragement for the future."

Our children are now nearly all in their forties, and we have three grandchildren, so you can imagine that a great deal of water has gone under the bridge since I first wrote those words!

My journal is hand-written (I'm old school!) and I store the pages in ring binders, of which there are now four! This means I can add cuttings, printed articles, etc, in plastic sleeves that I wish to keep for posterity! I don't journal every day – only when there is something significant to record, so I can sometimes go for a month without entering anything, and then perhaps find I'm writing in it every day for a short period. In it, I record situations I may be facing; scriptures and other ways in which the Lord is speaking; and some of my prayers. I also note any words or prophecies that folk have given us over the years – in fact, I've typed them up in a separate folder as it's key to keep on claiming those promises and rejoice when they come to be!

Over the years, God has been very gracious in giving me promises, particularly with regard to our children, and it has been immensely encouraging to re-read these words from time to time, linking them together to form a story of God's faithfulness to me and to His word. When I've committed my feelings – both happy and despairing – to paper, I can testify to the fact that when we turn to God, He provides us with exactly the kind of support and help we need at precisely the right time.

Recently, I felt God wanted me to study the Song of Songs to learn in greater depth of His love for me. This I have done in conjunction with a book called "The Sacred Journey", and I've been using a separate hardback journal for those notes as I want to be able to refer to them easily. However, I continue my "general" journal alongside that.

Because I've been journaling for so long, I don't often read back over it, unless there's a specific situation I want to be reminded of. Interestingly, when I recently felt prompted to start writing, my first book came about as a suggestion from a dear friend who encouraged me to look back through my journal, and note any significant lessons I had learnt – if only as a legacy for my children. It was fascinating reading back through so many years and being reminded of God's faithfulness; of His wonderful support particularly through tough times; and how often He used scripture to encourage me. I called the book "One More Step" (the oldies amongst you will remember the song "One more step along the way I go"), as it reflected the fact that God grows us one step at a time into greater maturity.

I'm sure I'm not alone when I say that I would very definitely not remember all the times God has interacted with me in significant ways that have changed my life unless I had my journal to refer to! In difficult times, it has helped remind me of His faithfulness and sustaining power, and it bears testimony to the ways God has spoken into my life – which in turn has been something I've been able to draw on in supporting others. It's such a part of my life now that I can't imagine not keeping one!

If you've not kept a journal, then I highly recommend you prayerfully give it consideration, finding a time in the day that suits you (for me it's mostly early morning). I promise you won't regret it! And if you're already keeping one, then don't give up – you'll be thrilled to look back and see the path on which God has taken you.

It may be you are working full-time in a demanding job, or you're at home with a family to look after. Either way, the thought of journaling can seem daunting. I can't quite remember how I found the time when our family was small or when I eventually went back to work, and even now I'm retired, life can still be very busy. But there's a song

with the line *"I find space for what I treasure, I find time for what I want, I choose my priorities, and Jesus You're my number one"*. *What God imparts to us on a personal level over the years will prove of more value than anything else in life.*

My husband and I use Phil Moore's "Straight to the Heart" series each morning together, and I was interested to read this in his exposition on Joshua chapter 4 (it can be quoted under "fair use" parameters!). I hope it encourages you in your journaling adventure.

"What are the major milestones on your own walk with God? I strongly encourage you to take some time to write a list of your own spiritual milestones. Forgetting is easy and remembering is hard, so don't miss the important lesson Joshua teaches us here. Joshua spurs us on by telling us in verse 9 that this particular pile of rocks was still there when the book was written. This is the first of twelve occasions when Joshua tells us that a spiritual marker is still "there to this day". Reflecting and recording the milestones in our journey with God takes time, but it is always worth the effort. The Lord chisels their memory so deeply into our hearts that they shape the way we view ourselves and what it means for us to follow him."

I hope you feel inspired to either start or continue with journaling and as time goes by, I pray that what you record will help you recognise the goodness of the Lord in your life and encourage you as you trust Him for your future. Make this your prayer: "Lord, direct me throughout my journey so I can experience your plans for my life. Reveal the life paths that are pleasing to you. Escort me along the way; take me by the hand and teach me." (Psalm 25:4-5 TPT)

Marion Palmer (retired)

Born in 1951, Marion grew up in a church-going family and accepted Jesus as her Saviour in her teens, although the need for His Lordship followed later in 1975. She met and married Barry in 1977 and they have three adult children and three grandchildren currently. She and Barry have been members of Hope Church Orpington since 1995, serving in a variety of capacities, in particular in the area of marriage and family life. In retirement, she has found new interests in the area of art and writing.

Conclusion

I hope you enjoyed reading about how journaling has impacted these amazing women. You might be thinking: "Oh wow, some of these ladies started journaling at a young age, no wonder they are very comfortable with journaling". It is not when you start that matters, what counts is that you begin.

All six women seem to agree that if you have never journaled or are considering journaling, all you have to do is start. Start small, and let it flow from there.

If you have journaled in the past but stopped, I want to encourage you to start again. I have a feeling you experienced the benefits of journaling then, but probably due to the demands and pressures of life, you abandoned journaling due to time constraints.

It is not too late to pick up the habit of journaling again! It will provide clarity to the different challenges you might be facing.

Journaling gives you a record of how you dealt with any issue, and how God came through for you. Having this reminder is so profound because you have the confidence to face any future challenges head-on because you have evidence of supernatural help from above in YOUR past.

To round off, I would like to share two hesitations some may have to journaling and my suggestions to address them.

#1. Fear someone else would read what they wrote.

In the survey, one reason many listed for not keeping a journal was the fear that someone else might read the contents of the journal…especially if the contents are raw. To them I would suggest:

- Always carry your journal around with you. If it is with you, no one else is likely to read it.
- If you work outside the home, keep it in a safe place where no one will see it.

Also, along that same line, if you want to write about something that you don't want anyone else to read, (such as frustration with your husband, child or friend), another suggestion would be to:

1. Write it all out on a sheet of paper.
2. Get the lesson from the experience.
3. Transfer the lesson to your journal.
4. Then, tear up or burn the piece of paper.

There is no value in risking your relationships over the content of your journal if they were mistakenly read by someone else.

#2 Thinking they don't have time to journal

Another common obstacle respondents of the survey wrote was finding the time to journal. Based on what you have read so far, I hope by now you know how valuable journaling is. So, if it is that beneficial and can help you in your life, accept my challenge to examine how you currently spend your time and see where you can fit in journaling. Even just a few minutes a day to get you started!

I typically journal during my time with God in the morning, so my suggestion is for you to do something similar. Incorporate journaling into your special time with God, whether it is in the morning, afternoon or evening. If you don't have a time you meet with God, I highly recommend you set a time now.

For you to live victoriously as a daughter of God, you can't afford to not spend time with your heavenly Father. In my book, Super Working Mum, I talk about maximising your morning and how to get up early. You can find that book on Amazon.

That's it! Remember, all you need to get started is a notebook and a pen. So start journaling today! :)

Recommended Journals

I would love to share with you some journals I have personally designed myself and other journals designed by women in the Super Working Mum community.

I hope that you will find one that suits your needs especially if you are just starting out. You can also get a combination of the below for yourself or as a gift for a loved one.

The Living Amazed By Everyday Miracles Journal

This book was written as a result of creating this journal. The Living Amazed journal is designed to help you journal for at least 5 to 10 minutes every day for at least 90 days.

It has guided prompts that will unlock your creative juices on recording your gratitude, prayers, and intentions for the day. The Living Amazed journal also has a section for free-flow writing.

By using this journal you will experience a paradigm shift in your life. You will always be aware of the goodness of God in your life despite your circumstances. You will sense God's presence and love for you always. You can get this journal by scanning the QR code.

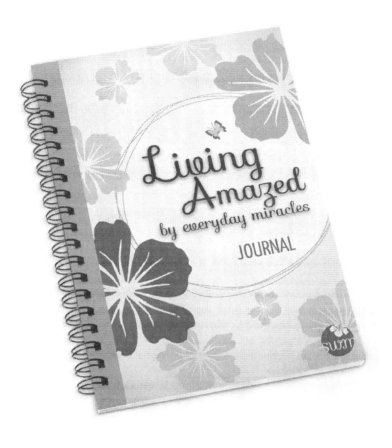

The Living Amazed By
Everyday Miracles Journal

The Living Purposefully Journal (Time Boxing Edition)

This is a 90 day productivity journal that allows you to set goals and plan on a quarterly, monthly, weekly and daily basis.

It is said that "What you don't schedule won't happen". This journal allows you to allocate 30 minute blocks of your day to the things that are important to you, making it more likely that they will get done. The ideal user for this productivity journal is someone:

1. *Who is busy.*
2. *Who has lots of big ideas, projects or goals and would like to break them down into bite size chunks that can be achieved quarterly.*
3. *Who could easily get distracted.*
4. *Who is likely a business owner or entrepreneur.*

This journal has been designed to help you to be more resolute, more determined and more intentional in your daily living. It also aims to help you keep track of what is important to you when you need to take that action, why you should take that action but how YOU actually execute the actions is up to you. You can get this journal by scanning the QR code.

Living

Purposefully

A 90-Day Productivity Journal

Timeboxing Edition

The Living Purposefully Journal (Time Boxing Edition)

The Living Purposefully Journal

This is the first 90-day productivity journal similar to the one above that allows you to set goals and plan on a quarterly, monthly, weekly and daily basis.

The main difference between this journal and the timeboxing edition is in the daily planning where you get to prioritise based on MUST Dos, Should Dos and Could Dos.

This journal was designed for anyone who gets overwhelmed or stressed out easily with all the various tasks they need to do. By using this journal you get to prioritise what is important to you and get them done. You can get this journal by scanning the QR code.

Living Purposefully
Purposefully
A 90-Day Productivity Journal

The Living
Purposefully Journal

A Companion Journal for Slay Doubt!

The Companion Journal for Slay Doubt! has been carefully designed to help you process and capture all that the Holy Spirit says to you during and after reading the book: "Slay Doubt: How to recognise and manifest God's calling on your life".

Through the guided reflective prompts and action steps from the Slay Doubt book, you will embark on a journey that will create awareness and propel you to take action so you can slay doubt.

As you take Holy spirit inspired action, you will likely experience transformation and the confidence to manifest God's calling on your life. This journal can be purchased on Amazon or by scanning the QR code.

A Companion
Journal for
Slay
Doubt!

How to recognise and
manifest God's calling
on your life

'Detola Amure

*A Companion Journal
for Slay Doubt!*

My Little Book of Big Prayers

This journal is a very helpful tool for recording your 'big' prayer points in one place and provides an opportunity to record the testimony of when and how that prayer has been answered. Doing this over and over will fire up your faith to dare to dream bigger and trust without hesitation.

There are also ten testimonies from friends who wanted to be a part of this project by sharing about how God stepped in and turned their situations around. Those testimonies are found every ten pages or so and are meant to encourage you to keep going as you ask, trust, and rejoice.

The Index page will help you to find the prayer quite quickly so you can record and date the answer to the prayer with an opportunity to write how that prayer was answered.

The journal has the opportunity to record up to 120 prayers and testimonies. Ongoing use will help this little book become a jewel of answered prayers in your hands.

"Truly I tell you, if you have faith as small as a mustard seed, you can say to this mountain, 'Move from here to there,' and it will move. Nothing will be impossible for you." - Matthew 17:20

This journal can be purchased on Amazon or by scanning the QR code.

My Little Book of
Big Prayers

Desired Not Abandoned (DNA) Journal

This is a journal to capture empowering words about yourself from the Father. You are who God says you are. What He says about you trumps anything less you believe or feel about yourself.

If the Father says you are desired, that means you have value. If He says you are not abandoned that means you are never on your own without Him. There is undeniable power in writing things down.

However those words come to you - the DNA journal has been designed to allow you to create a collection of reminders that speak to your value and most importantly your value in God's eyes. The journal also comes with some insights, poems and scriptures to get you going.

This journal can be purchased by scanning the QR code.

Desired Not Abandoned
(DNA) Journal

Unmask Your Beauty Journal for Teens

The Unmask Your Beauty Journal was created as a tool to help teenage girls cultivate their inner beauty and confidence through journaling. Journaling for the next 100 days will help teens develop a great habit of writing down their life experiences and most importantly take them on a journey of self-discovery.

The aim of the journal is to equip teens to identify themselves as valuable with much to contribute to society, build confidence & gain understanding of intrinsic value, understand that they are able to have a positive influence in their world and identify personal desires and strengths to motivate you to set and achieve personal goals.

This journal can be purchased by scanning the QR code.

Printed in Poland
by Amazon Fulfillment
Poland Sp. z o.o., Wrocław
01 June 2023

Write Read Run journal

The Write Read Run journal has been created to help you write your prophetic words in one place so that you can diligently review them while you faithfully await their fulfilment.

God loves to communicate with us and the Holy Spirit has been given to us to help us hear Him and the plans He has for us. One way those plans are revealed to us is through prophetic words.

With this Journal, you can date the prophetic word, where it was given, the name of the person who gave the word and record its fulfilment date. The index page allows you to reference the prophetic word so that you can quickly find a particular word whenever needed.

It is a tool to build and strengthen you in your faith journey. It can also aid your thanksgiving as it helps you recall what God has done. The journal gives the opportunity to record up to 120 individual prophetic words. Habakkuk 2:2 says, "Then the Lord answered me and said: Write the vision and make it plain on tablets, that he may run who reads it" (NKJV)

This journal is a practical tool to enable you to do just that.

This journal can be purchased on Amazon or by scanning the QR code.

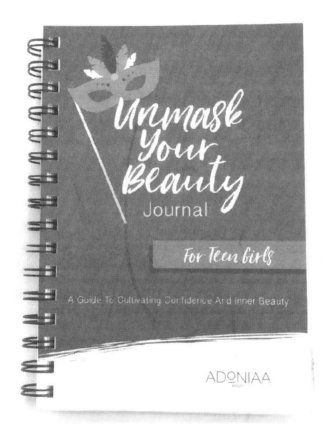

Unmask Your Beauty
Journal for Teens

Note from the Author

Write Read Run
journal

Thank you for buying this book. I would love it to be read by as many Christian women as possible, because I believe it will transform their minds and set them free from doubt and fear so they can confidently manifest God's calling on their lives.

If you enjoyed reading it, you can please help spread the word by doing the following

Recommend It. Suggest this book to other women in your circle of influence or buy it as a gift for others.

Talk About It. Mention it on Facebook, Twitter, or Instagram. Create a conversation about it using the hashtags #journaling #livingamazed #superworkingmum. You may also use the cover image as your profile picture on social networking sites.

Write About It. You can write about your thoughts from this book in an article or review it on your blog or someone's blog. Please email me at aloted@superworkingmum.com, when you do!

Discuss It. If you are part of a book club, recommend this book to be read in your book club and discuss the chapters.

Review It. Leave a review online. By leaving a review online, Amazon is likely to suggest this book to others to buy.

Many thanks for spreading the word.

About Super Working Mum

Super Working Mum (SWM) is a global organisation that aims to help Kingdom Women & Mothers who are overwhelmed MAXIMISE their time so that they can MANIFEST their God given dreams.

SWM help women to achieve the above through one or more of the following ways:

The Super Working Mum Community;
The Super Working Mum Academy;
The Super Working Mum Weekend Retreats;
The Digital Transformation Program for Super Working Mums ;
The Empowering Mothers Annual Conference in September;

For more information please visit www.superworkingmum.com.

TAKE THE MANIFEST DREAM QUIZ!

Ever felt stuck yet you know there is more to life?

To gain clarity, ditch overwhelm and live a purposeful life so you can say YES to what is important to you, scan the code to take the Manifest Your Dream Quiz.

Other books by 'Detola

| Super Working Mum | Slay Doubt! | Boosting Your Confidence |

All books are available on **Amazon**.

About Detola Amure

Detola is known to be an Encourager, Activator and Emancipator of Women. She is a Productivity Coach, Maxwell Leadership Certified Coach, Trainer & Speaker, Certified DISC Behavioural Trainer and an Advanced Grief Recovery Specialist.

She is the founder of Super Working Mum, a global organisation dedicated to helping Kingdom women & mothers who want to MAXIMISE their time so they can MANIFEST their God-given dreams.

She is the author of 3 other books- Amazon Best Sellers: *Super Working Mum*, *Slay Doubt!* and *Boosting Your Confidence*.

Detola is married with four children (one of them lives in heaven). She currently lives in Kent, UK with her family.

You can connect with her on www.detolamure.com and listen to her podcast, When Life Stops on www.whenlifestops.org